SECOND EDITION
MUSIC THEORY for Young Children

1

Name : . . . .

Address: . . . .

Phone : . . . .

YING YING NG

Published by:

pocostudio
MAKE SENSE OF MUSIC

Poco Studio Sdn Bhd (646228-V)
B-2-8, IOI Boulevard, Jalan Kenari 5, Bandar Puchong Jaya, 47170 Puchong, Selangor, Malaysia
Tel/Fax: +603 8074 0086 | Mobile: +6013-6185289 (WhatsApp) | Email: poco_studio@yahoo.co.uk | pocostudio.org | facebook.com/pocostudio

Copyright © 2004, 2014 by Poco Studio Sdn Bhd

Copyediting by David C L Ngo, MA, BAI, PhD, FIET, FBCS, SMIEEE

Printed in Malaysia

ISBN: 978-967-12504-0-2

Dear Teachers and Parents,

Music Theory for Young Children is a four-level young children music theory series, adapted from the Music Theory for Young Musicians series. Aiming to teach the fundamentals of music theory in a fun and novel way, it combines an exam-based syllabus, a child-centred approach to content development, and an interactive methodology to make an engaging and effective course for young music learners. Based on 10 years of market-tested and -refined methods, the new and revised content, fresh new look, appealing illustrations and stickers, and a variety of self-motivating exercises make it the perfect series for encouraging a child's interest in music and developing their knowledge. We hope for your continued support in the future.

Best Wishes,
Ying Ying Ng

What the experts say…

Music Theory for Young Children, a step-by-step series of four music theory books, will be welcomed by teachers and parents who are fully aware of the importance of a sound theoretical foundation in support of practical music studies. From Beginners to Grade 1 each new element is introduced and explored by means of an inventive system of activities which is guaranteed to appeal to young children. The series is also designed to provide a progressive revision course for music students of all ages.

I have pleasure in recommending this series as an exciting new approach to the early stages of music education, and congratulate Ying Ying Ng on her achievement.

Ita Beausang BMus MA PhD LRAM
Former Acting Director, Lecturer in Musicianship Studies
DIT Conservatory of Music and Drama, Dublin, Ireland

That Ying-Ying Ng's new series of theory books for children is not only innovative and attractive, but also pedagogically sound, is no surprise. Ying-Ying was awarded a Special Commendation in Teaching at her final examinations at the DIT Conservatory of Music and Drama. This award recognises exceptional talent in communicating ideas and in motivating students.

The more formal, traditional music theory book can certainly act as a de-motivating force for children. I would love to be a child again and to learn music theory in such a "fun" way! I have no hesitation in wholeheartedly endorsing the series.

Margaret O'Sullivan Farrell BMus DipMus LTCL
Course Director, Lecturer in Keyboard Studies
DIT Conservatory of Music and Drama, Dublin, Ireland

CONTENTS

Paste the black keys.

The keyboard is made up of groups of 2 black keys and groups of 3 black keys.

Circle each group of 2 black keys. **Trace** the letter names C D E.

Circle each group of 3 black keys. **Trace** the letter names F G A B.

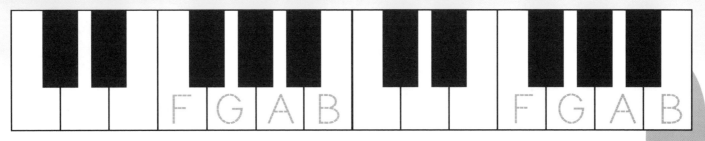

Trace and **paste** the letter names.

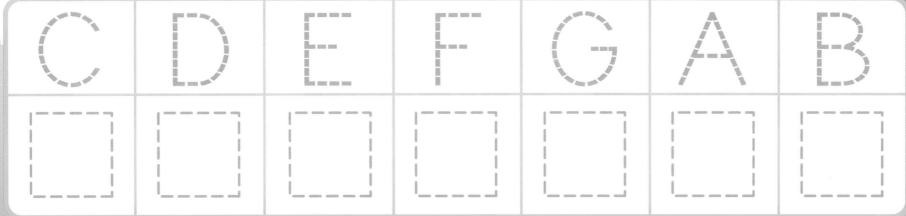

C D E F G A B

Letter Names

Paste the letter name in each box.

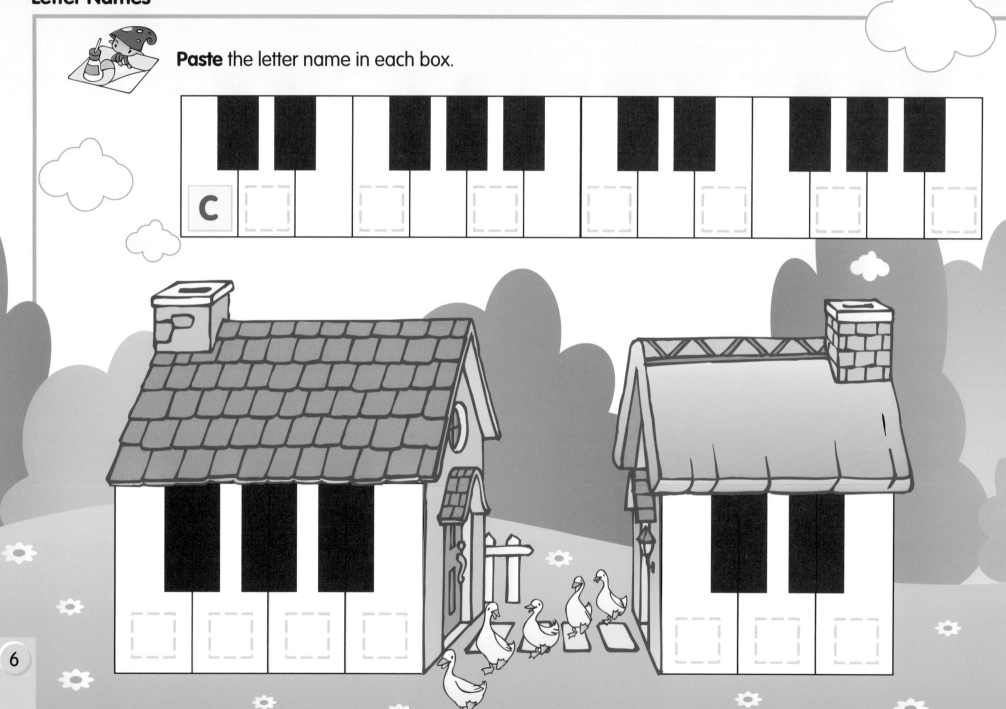

C

Paste the letter name for each coloured key.

Paste the missing letter names.

C D E ● ● A B

C D ● ● G ● B

F ● A ● C ● E

F G ● B ● ● E

8

Trace and **write** the letter names.

C D E F G A B

9

Trace the clefs. Colour the number on each finger.

left hand

right hand

bass clef

treble clef

Trace your left hand and right hand and **paste** the number on each finger.

left hand

right hand

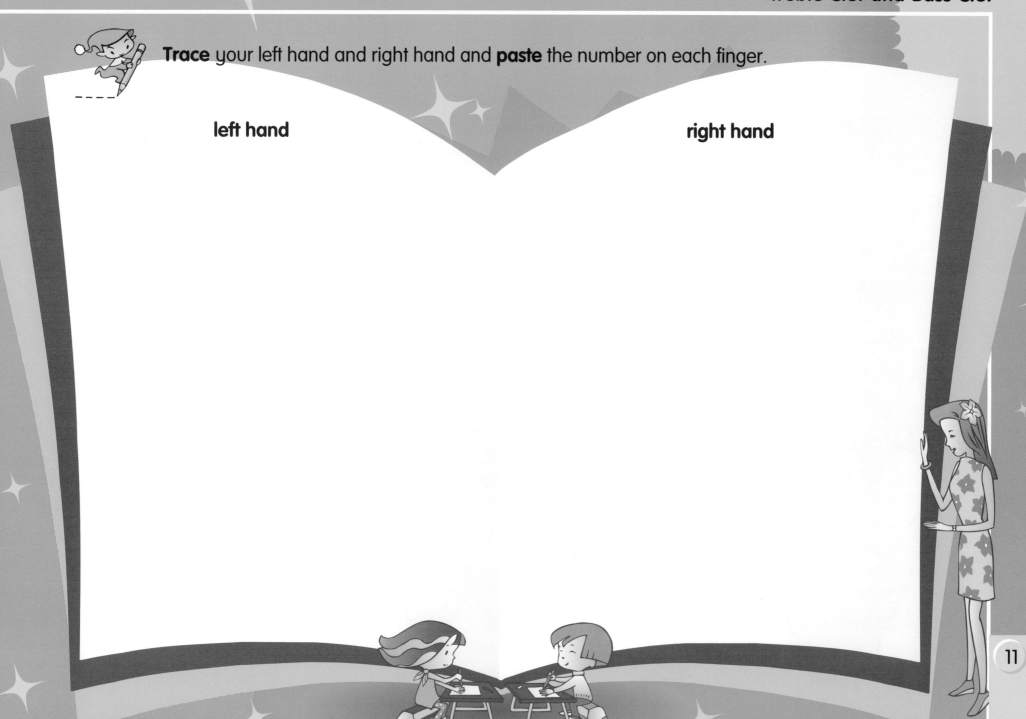

Treble Clef and Bass Clef

Paste the clef for each hand.

12

Trace the treble clefs.

Trace the bass clefs.

Paste the clefs.

bass clef

treble clef

bass clef

treble clef

13

Time Names and Time Values

Paste the time values.

Time Name	semibreve (whole note)	minim (half note)	crotchet (quarter note)
Note	𝅝	𝅗𝅥	♩
Time Value			

Circle the correct notes.

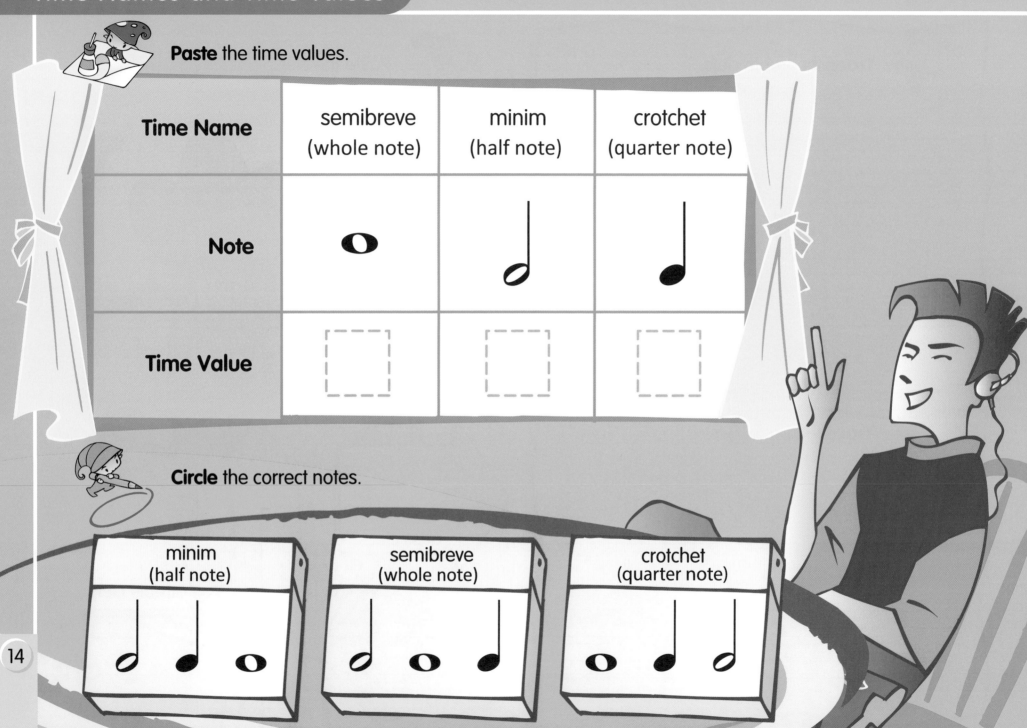

| minim (half note) | semibreve (whole note) | crotchet (quarter note) |

Colour the same notes in each box.

15

Trace the notes and time names.

semibreve
(whole note)

semibreve
(whole note)

minim
(half note)

minim
(half note)

crotchet
(quarter note)

crotchet
(quarter note)

Paste the notes and time names.

minim
(half note)

Time Names and Time Values

For each note, **circle** the number of flowers that match the time value and **paste** the time name.

semibreve
(whole note)

Colour the correct time value for each note.

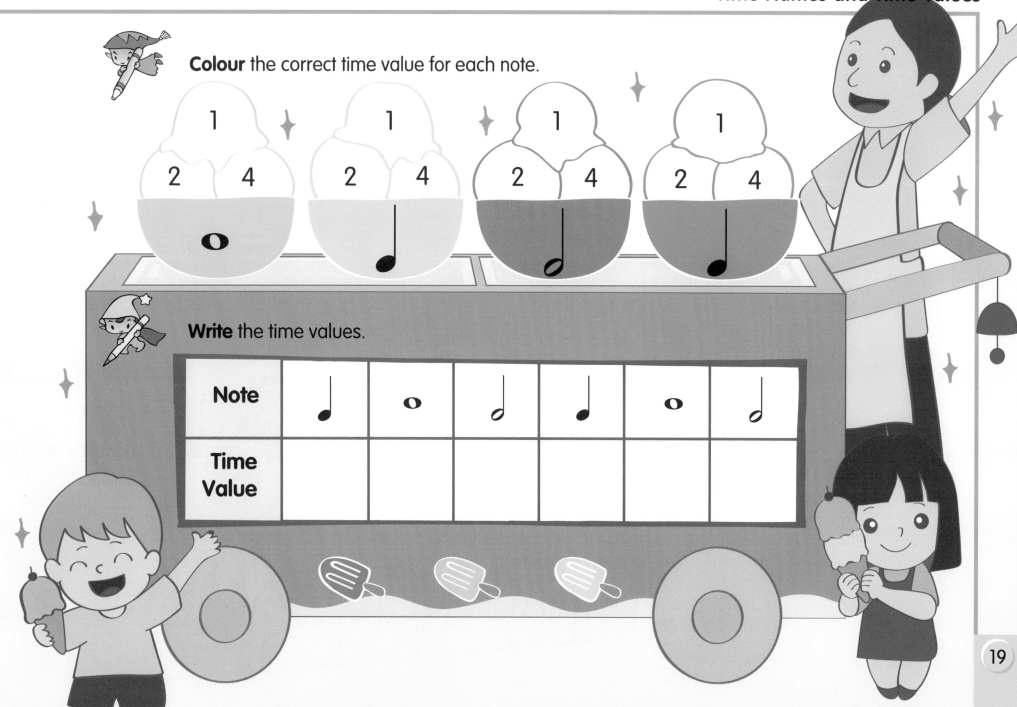

Write the time values.

Note	♩	𝅝	♩	♩	𝅝	♪
Time Value						

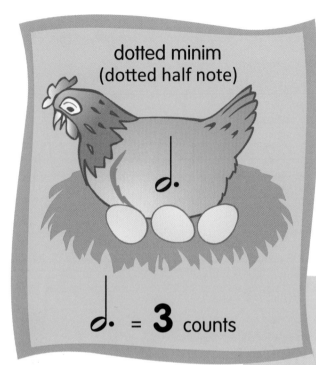

dotted minim
(dotted half note)

♩. = **3** counts

Trace the dotted minims
(dotted half notes).

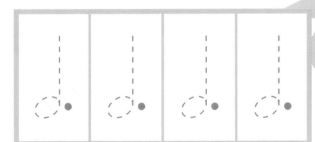

Paste the number of eggs that match the time value of each note.

Colour the corrrect notes.

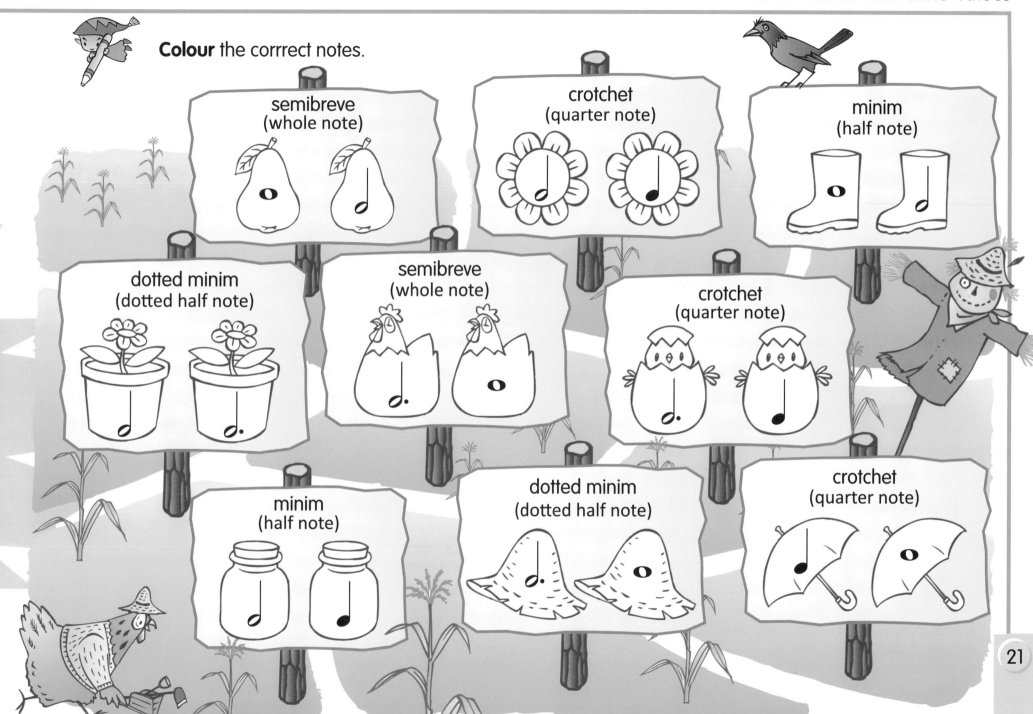

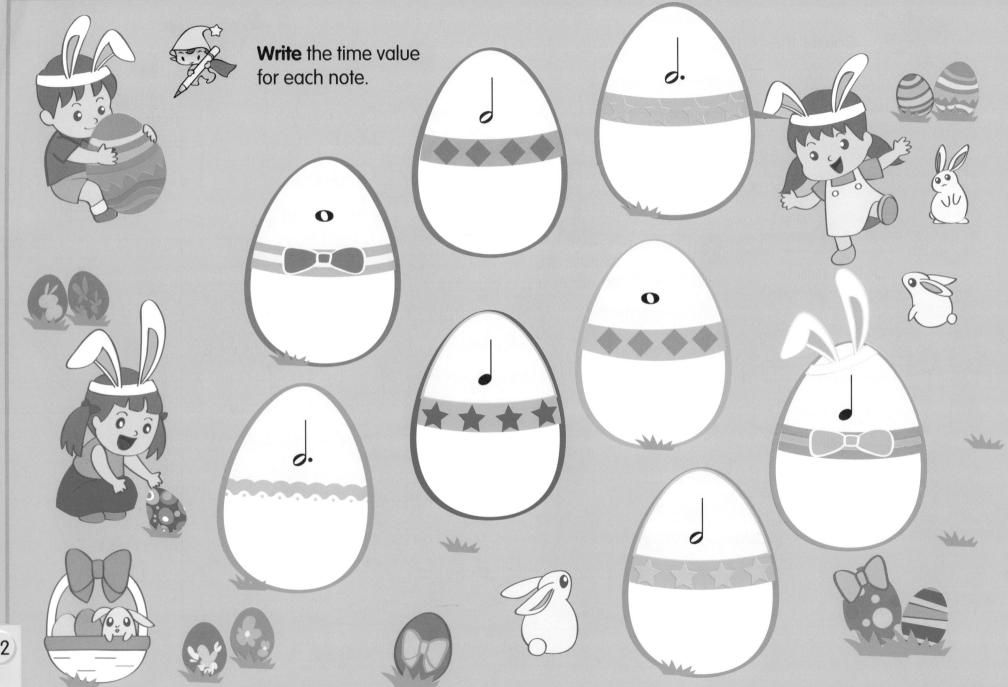

Write the time value for each note.

Circle the longest notes.

Circle the shortest notes.

Paste the notes from longest to shortest.

Paste the notes from shortest to longest.

Time Names and Time Values

Trace and **copy** the time names.

o	d.	d	♩
semibreve (whole note)	dotted minim (dotted half note)	minim (half note)	crotchet (quarter note)
semibreve (whole note)	dotted minim (dotted half note)	minim (half note)	crotchet (quarter note)

Colour the correct time name for each note.

crotchet
(quarter note)

cortchet
(qurater note)

doteed minim
(doteed half note)

dotted minim
(dotted half note)

mimim
(hafl note)

minim
(half note)

semibreve
(whole note)

seimbreve
(whelo note)

25

Time Names and Time Values

Write the time name and time value for each note.

Colour the picture using the code.

2 counts

3 counts

4 counts

Paste 2 line notes on every line.

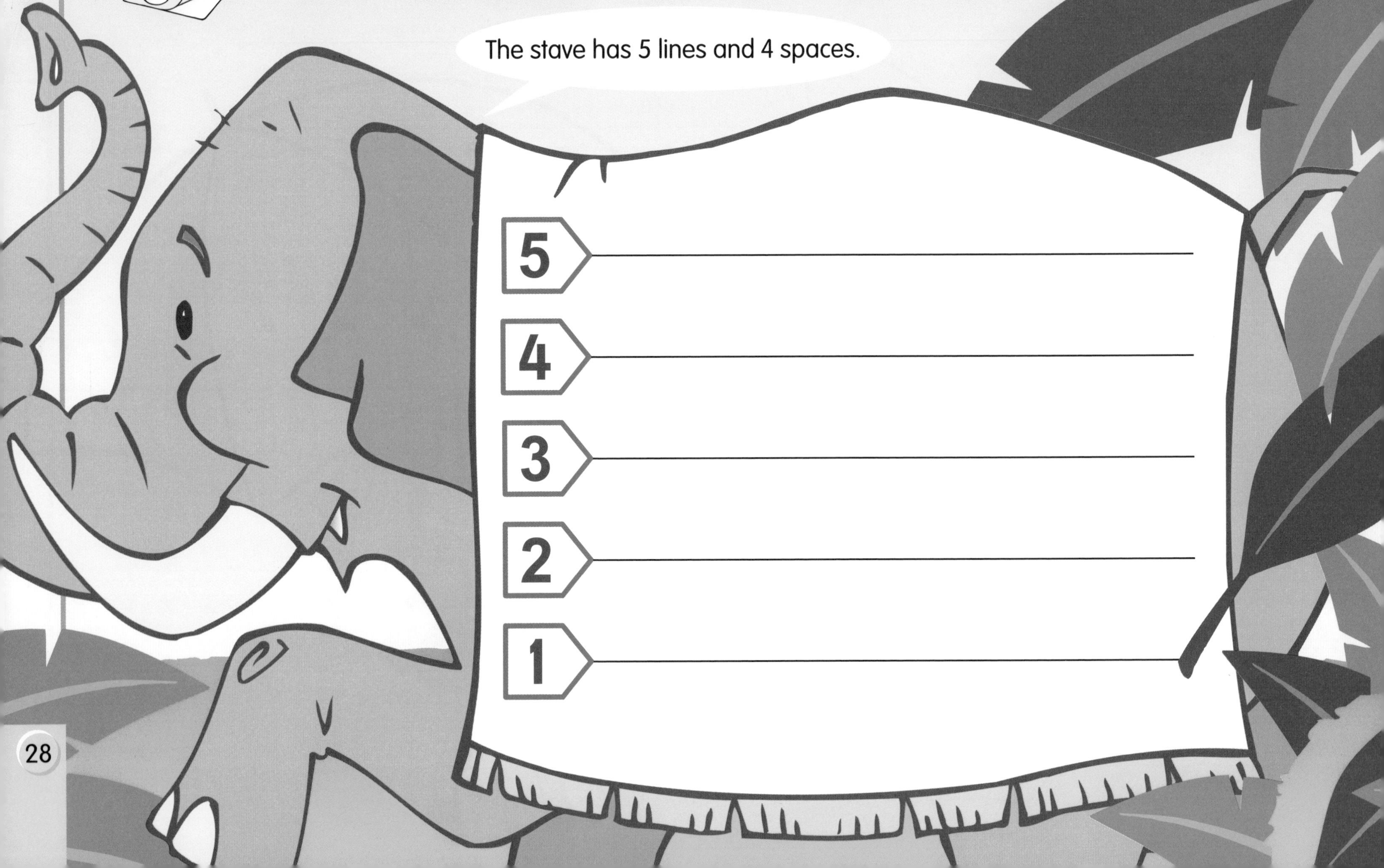

The stave has 5 lines and 4 spaces.

5

4

3

2

1

Paste 2 space notes in every space.

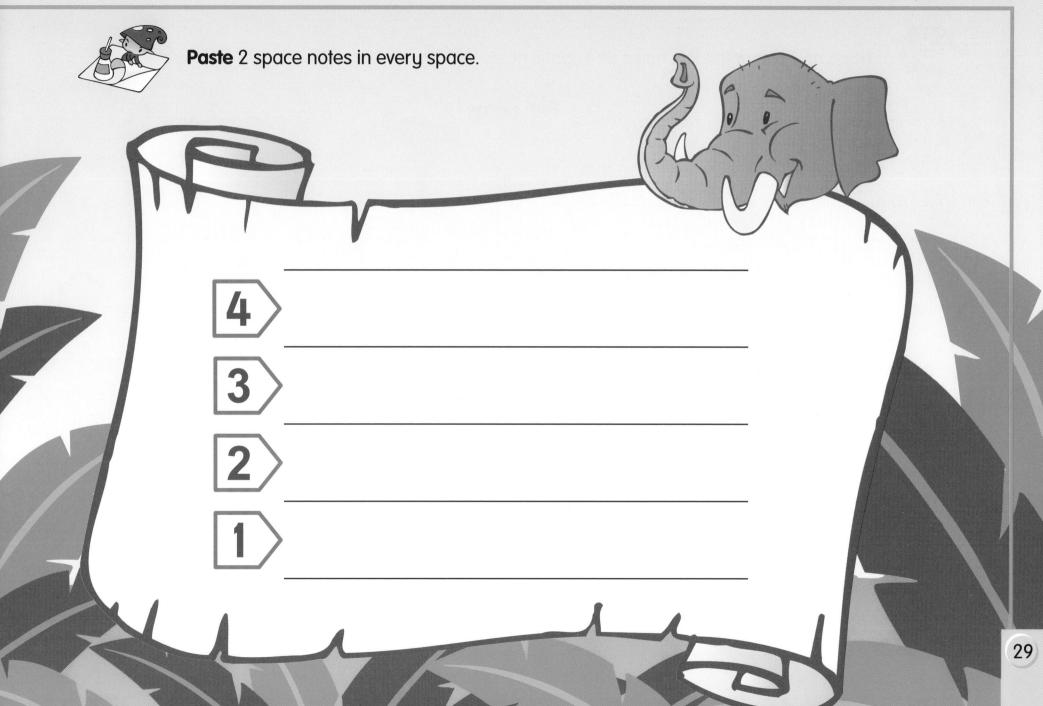

Line Notes and Space Notes

Trace and **colour** the line notes and space notes.

line notes

space notes

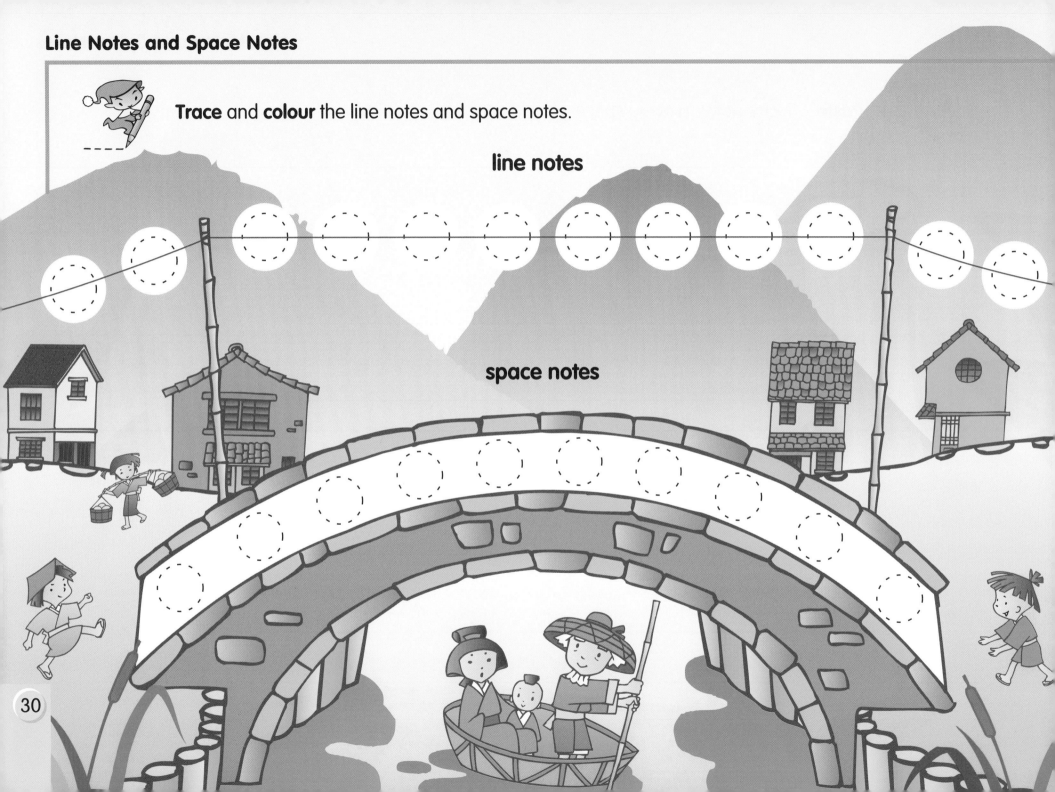

line notes

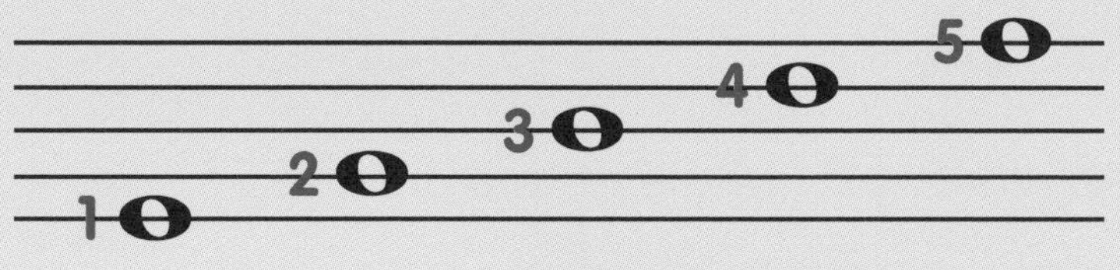
1
2
3
4
5

space notes

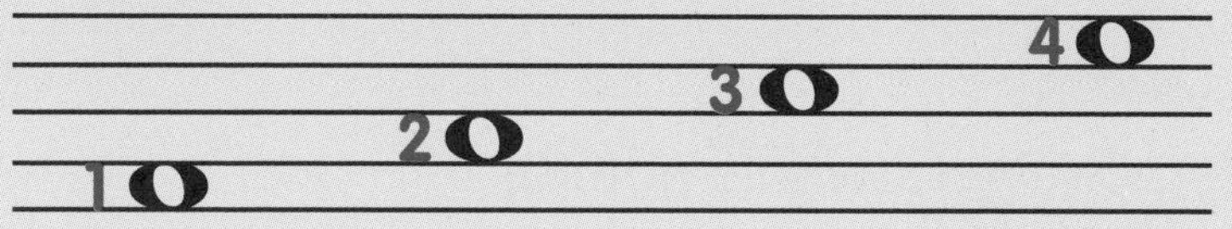
1
2
3
4

Write the notes as semibreves (whole notes).

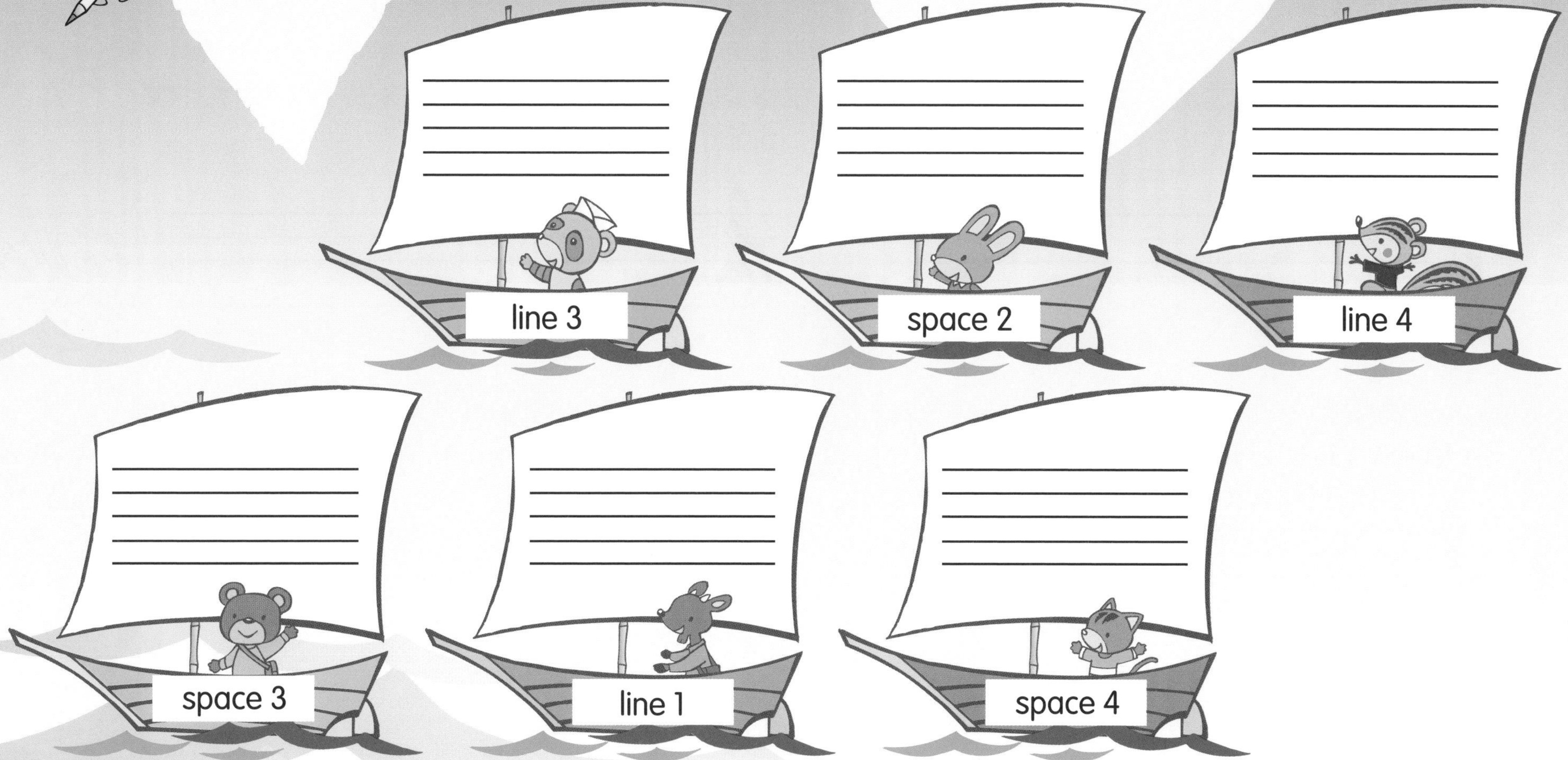
line 3
space 2
line 4
space 3
line 1
space 4

Treble Clef Notes

Trace and **write** the notes.

semibreve C (whole note C)

C

semibreve D (whole note D)

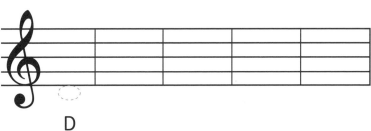

D

minim C (half note C)

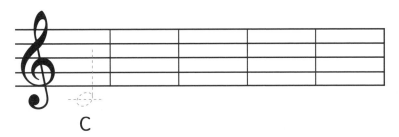

C

minim D (half note D)

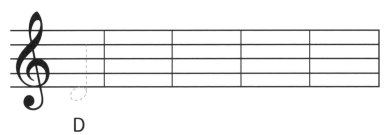

D

crotchet C (quarter note C)

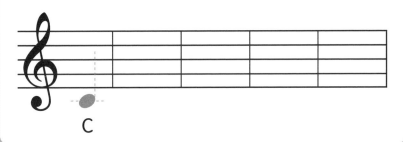

C

crotchet D (quarter note D)

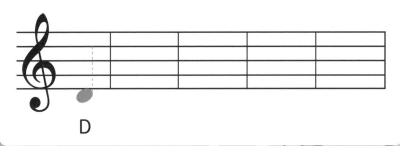

D

Colour the note C.

Colour the note D.

Paste the notes.

semibreve D
(whole note D)

crotchet C
(quarter note C)

minim D
(half note D)

dotted minim C
(dotted half note C)

33

Trace and **write** the notes.

semibreve E (whole note E)

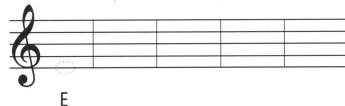

E

minim E (half note E)

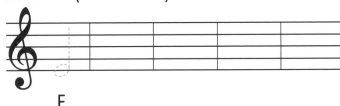

E

crotchet E (quarter note E)

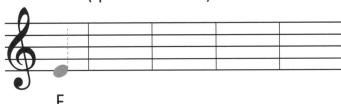

E

Colour the note E.

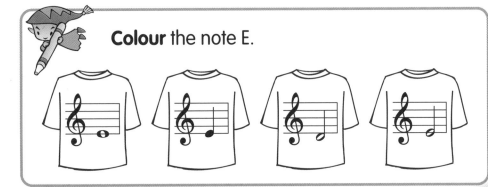

Draw a line to match each note group with the correct letter name group.

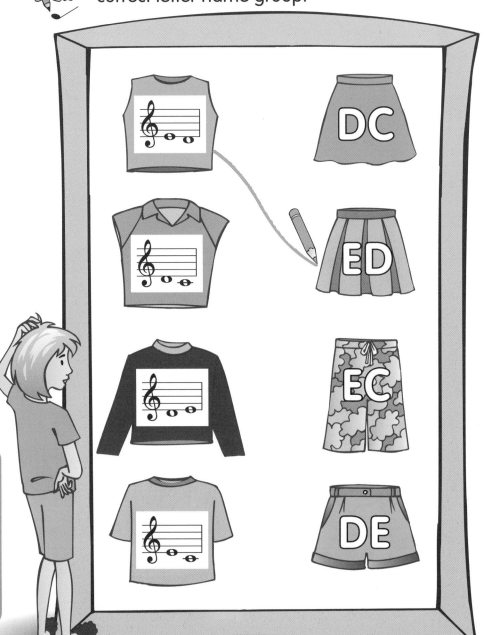

Write the notes as semibreves (whole notes).

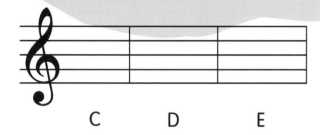

C   D   E

Write the notes as minims (half notes).

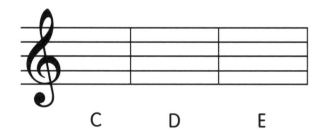

C   D   E

Write the notes as crotchets (quarter notes).

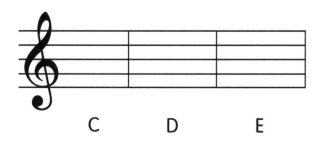

C   D   E

Colour the correct time name and letter name for each note.

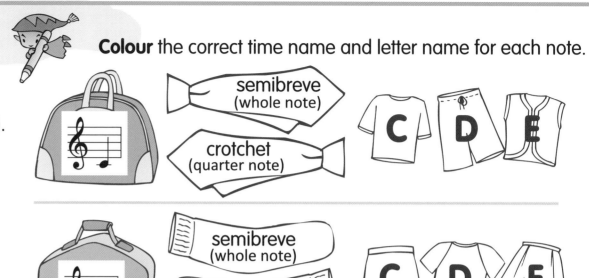

semibreve (whole note)

crotchet (quarter note)

C   D   E

semibreve (whole note)

minim (half note)

C   D   E

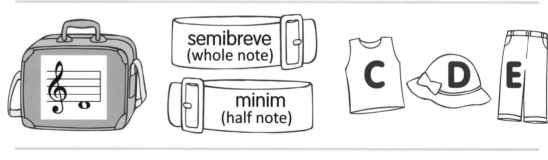

semibreve (whole note)

minim (half note)

C   D   E

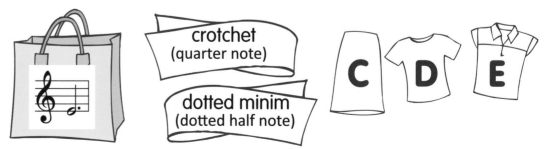

crotchet (quarter note)

dotted minim (dotted half note)

C   D   E

35

Treble Clef Notes

Trace and **write** the notes.

semibreve F (whole note F)

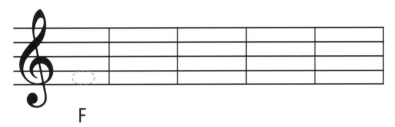

F

semibreve G (whole note G)

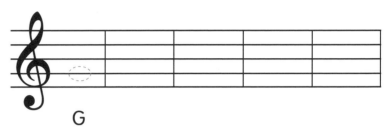

G

minim F (half note F)

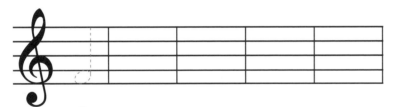

F

minim G (half note G)

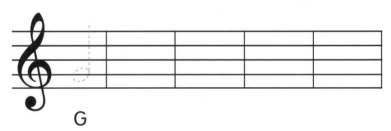

G

crotchet F (quarter note F)

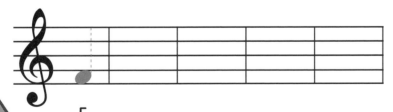

F

crotchet G (quarter note G)

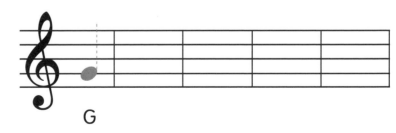

G

Paste stickers in the correct boxes.

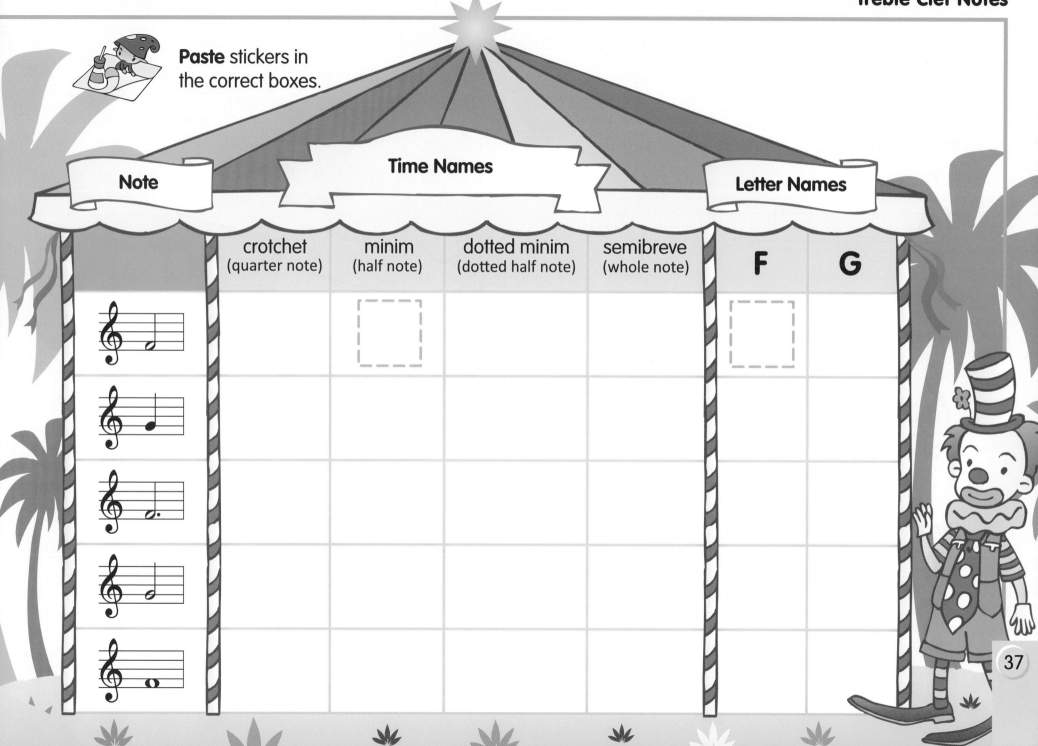

Note	Time Names				Letter Names	
	crotchet (quarter note)	minim (half note)	dotted minim (dotted half note)	semibreve (whole note)	F	G

37

Treble Clef Notes

Write the notes as semibreves (whole notes).

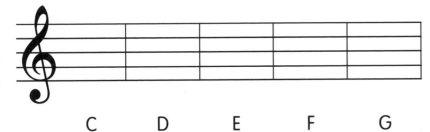

C   D   E   F   G

Write the notes as minims (half notes).

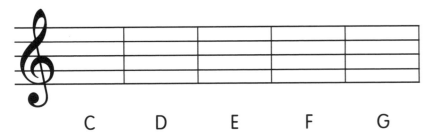

C   D   E   F   G

Write the notes as crotchets (quarter notes).

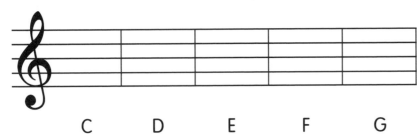

C   D   E   F   G

Circle the correct letter name for each note.

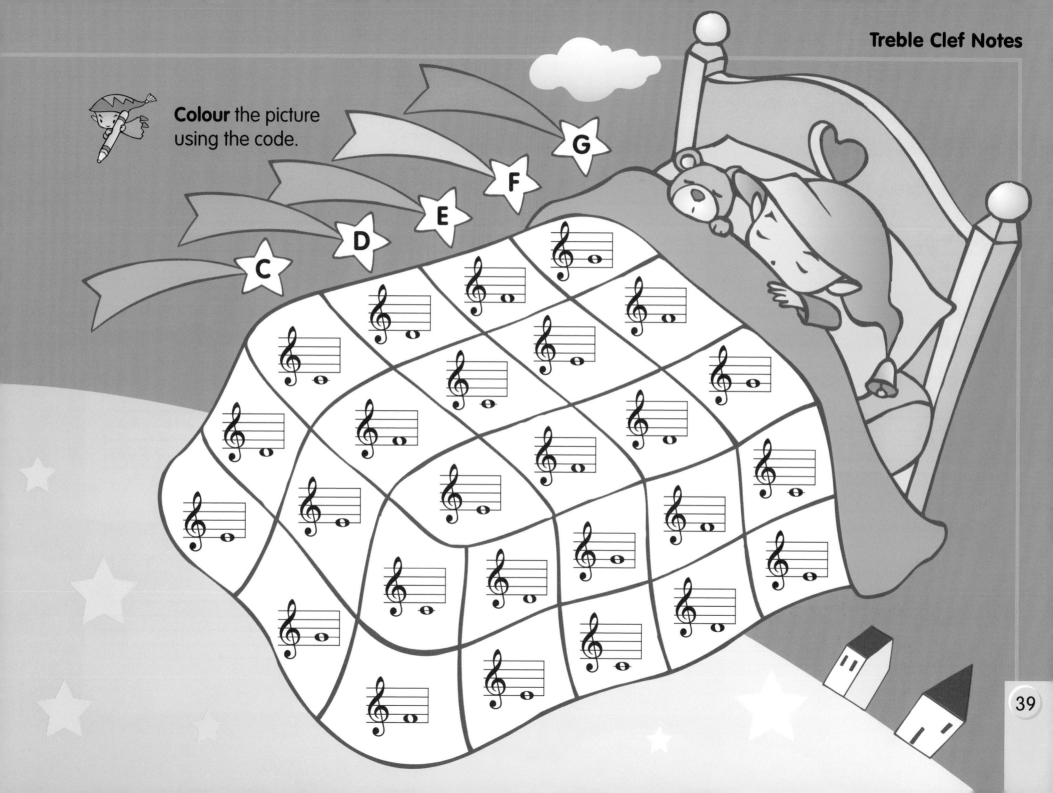

Colour the picture using the code.

Bass Clef Notes

 Trace and **write** the notes.

semibreve C (whole note C)

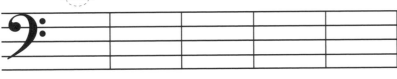

C

semibreve B (whole note B)

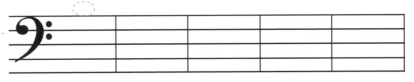

B

minim C (half note C)

C

minim B (half note B)

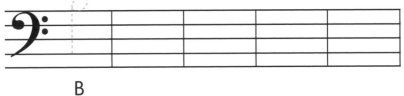

B

crotchet C (quarter note C)

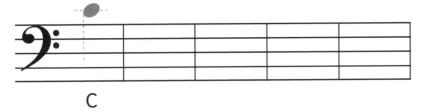

C

crotchet B (quarter note B)

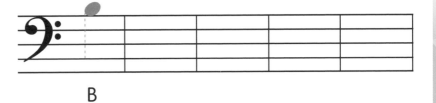

B

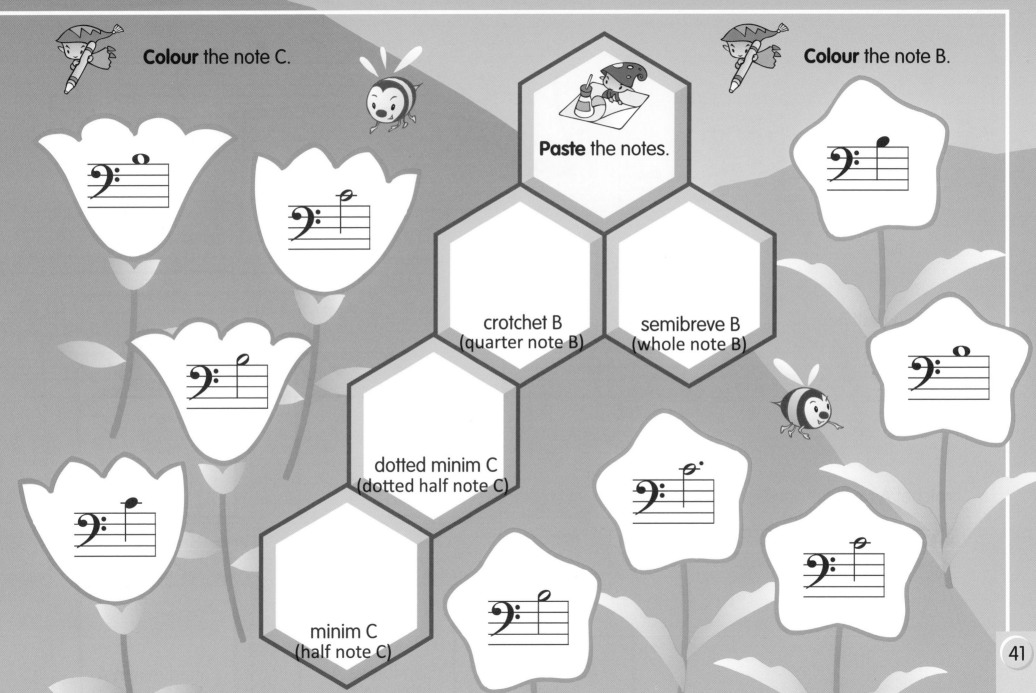

Colour the note C.

Paste the notes.

Colour the note B.

crotchet B
(quarter note B)

semibreve B
(whole note B)

dotted minim C
(dotted half note C)

minim C
(half note C)

41

Bass Clef Notes

Trace and **write** the notes.

semibreve A (whole note A)

A

minim A (half note A)

A

crotchet A (quarter note A)

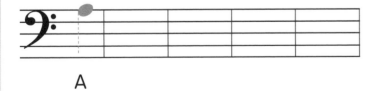

A

Circle the note A.

Paste the notes.

minim A
(half note A)

crotchet A
(quarter note A)

semibreve A
(whole note A)

dotted minim A
(dotted half note A)

Colour the correct key for each note.

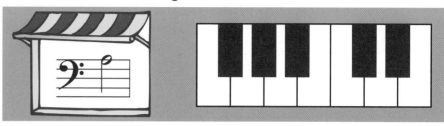

Write the notes as semibreves (whole notes).

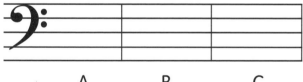

A   B   C

Write the notes as minims (half notes).

A   B   C

Write the notes as crotchets (quarter notes).

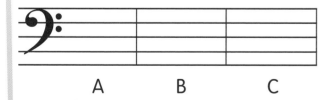

A   B   C

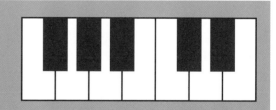

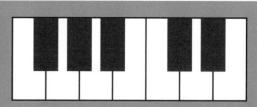

43

Bass Clef Notes

Trace and **write** the notes.

G
semibreve G (whole note G)

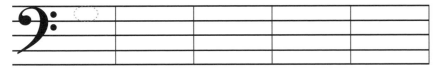

G

semibreve F (whole note F)

F

minim G (half note G)

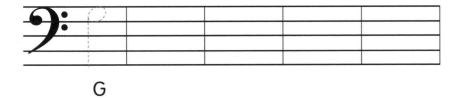

G

minim F (half note F)

F

crotchet G (quarter note G)

G

crotchet F (quarter note F)

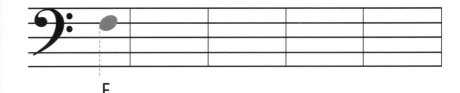

F

Paste the letter name and time value for each note.

Write the notes as semibreves (whole notes).

F　　　G　　　A　　　B　　　C

Write the notes as minims (half notes).

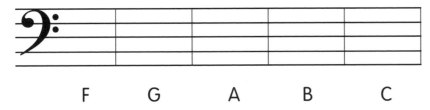

F　　　G　　　A　　　B　　　C

Write the notes as crotchets (quarter notes).

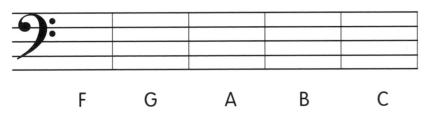

F　　　G　　　A　　　B　　　C

Write the notes.

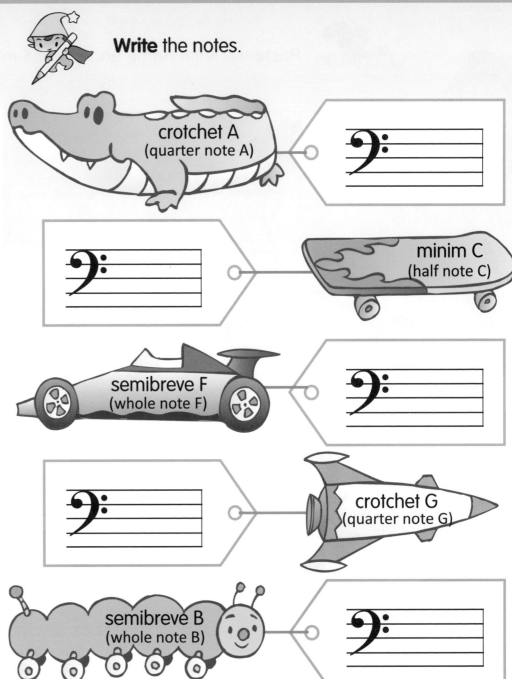

Colour the picture using the code.

Candy Shop

C
B
A
G
F

Bass Clef Notes

Paste the correct clefs.

1. **Write** the notes as semibreves. /20

 /100

 C

 C

 E

 G

 D

 G

 F

 A

 F

 B

100 ⭐⭐⭐⭐⭐
90 ⭐⭐⭐⭐
80 ⭐⭐⭐
70 ⭐⭐
60 ⭐

2. **Circle** the correct time value for each note. /12

♩ 1 2 3 4

♩ 1 2 3 4

♩. 1 2 3 4

𝅝 1 2 3 4

Assessment

3. For each question, **circle** the lowest note and **write** the letter name. 12

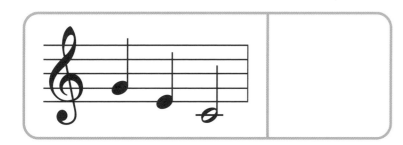

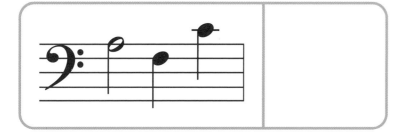

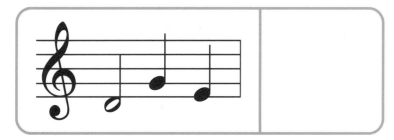

4. For each question, **circle** the highest note and **write** the letter name. 12

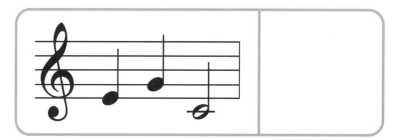

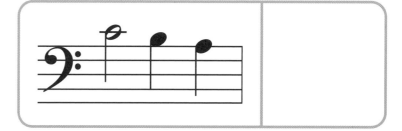

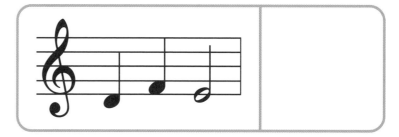

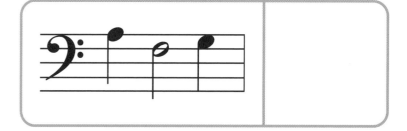

5. **Write** the notes. 20

crotchet E
(quarter note E)

minim D
(half note D)

crotchet G
(quarter note G)

semibreve F
(whole note F)

minim C
(half note C)

minim B
(half note B)

crotchet F
(quarter note F)

minim G
(half note G)

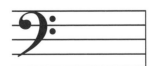
crotchet A
(quarter note A)

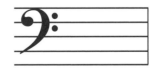
semibreve C
(whole note C)

6. **Fill in** the blanks with the given words. ⬜/24

stave	treble clef	clefs	bass clef
crotchet (quarter note)	semibreve (whole note)	dotted minim (dotted half note)	minim (half note)